ca. 1440

The printing press is invented in Europe. Books spread rapidly.

2016

For the first time, a tool is 3-D printed in outer space. It is a multi-tool, including a wedge.

1763

James Watt begins developing a steam engine that can drive a piston.

ca. 1000 CE

The spinning wheel is invented in India, making it much easier to make yarn and fabric.

1760–1830

The Industrial Revolution sees a huge increase in mechanization, with machines introduced in many industries.

1879

Karl Benz patents an internal combustion engine and uses it to power a car.

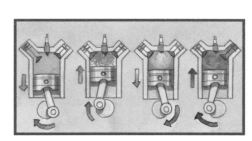

Origins of Simple Machines

United States:
3-D printer

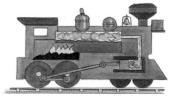

Scotland:
Steam engine

Iraq: Archimedes' screw

China and
Iran: Windmills

Iraq, Georgia
(Eurasia):
Wheels used for
transportation

Africa: Earliest
humans use levers
and wedges

India:
Spinning wheel

Germany: Internal
combustion engine

China: Wedges
used as plows

It's impossible to say exactly where some simple machines were first used, because they are so fundamental, they are even used by animals. Wedges, along with sticks used as simple levers, were probably used by the earliest humans about 185,000 years ago.

Other simple machines were first used at about the same time in different places around the world. It is only in the case of more advanced machines, comprising several parts, that we have a better idea of where and when they were first used.

Author:

Anne Rooney has a PhD in English from the University of Cambridge. She is the author of many books for children and adults, specializing in science and technology topics.

Artist:

Mark Bergin was born in Hastings, England, in 1961. He studied at Eastbourne College of Art and specializes in historical reconstructions, aviation, and maritime subjects. He lives in Bexhill-on-Sea with his wife and children.

Editor: **Jonathan Ingoldby**

Editorial Assistant: **Mark Williams**

PAPER FROM
SUSTAINABLE
FORESTS

Published in Great Britain in 2019 by
The Salariya Book Company Ltd
25 Marlborough Place, Brighton BN1 1UB

Library of Congress Cataloging-in-Publication Data
Names: Rooney, Anne, author. | Bergin, Mark, 1961- illustrator.
Title: You wouldn't want to live without simple machines! / written by Anne Rooney ; illustrated by Mark Bergin.
Description: New York : Franklin Watts, an imprint of Scholastic Inc., [2018] Includes bibliographical references and index.
Identifiers: LCCN 2018006930| ISBN 9780531128152 (library binding) | ISBN 9780531193631 (pbk.)
Subjects: LCSH: Simple machines--Juvenile literature.
Classification: LCC TJ147 .R656 2018 | DDC 621.8--dc23 LC record available at https://lccn.loc.gov/2018006930

All rights reserved.
Published in 2019 in the United States
by Franklin Watts
An imprint of Scholastic Inc.

Printed and bound in China.
Printed on paper from sustainable sources.
1 2 3 4 5 6 7 8 9 10 R 28 27 26 25 24 23 22 21 20 19

You Wouldn't Want to Live Without™

Simple Machines!

Written by
Anne Rooney

Illustrated by
Mark Bergin

Franklin Watts®
An Imprint of Scholastic Inc.

Contents

Introduction

Simple machines are around us all the time, and we use them every day, often without thinking. Some of them are so simple you probably don't even recognize them as machines. How about a knife? A hammer? Tweezers? They all count as *simple machines*! Many simple machines are hiding inside complex devices, called *compound machines*—but the simple machines are still in there, doing their job. You'd be surprised at how many simple machines you use every day—you really wouldn't want to live without them.

This pizza cutter makes it so much easier.

What Is a Machine?

A machine is a mechanical device, or tool, that uses energy to control or produce movement. That might sound rather complicated, but it just means that a machine is something that helps you to move things. To be useful, a machine must make a task easier. It does this by amplifying—increasing the effect of—a force. Machines can be simple—working on just one type of force or movement—or complicated.

MORE COMPLICATED machines, such as car engines, are known as compound machines. They incorporate many, many simple machines working together.

TO SCIENTISTS, *work* has a very specific meaning: It's the energy it takes to exert a force over a distance. That means thinking about a hard math problem isn't work, but playing soccer is!

Your body works like a machine: It takes energy from food and uses it to do "work" with your muscles. It has lots of parts that work as simple machines.

MOVEMENT is produced and controlled by forces (pushes or pulls). If we know the forces involved, we can figure out just how an object will move. Often, there are several forces working at once—it can get tricky!

A MACHINE increases the effect of a force. But it can't reduce the work needed to do a task. It swaps things around: You can move a small load farther, or a larger load a short distance, for example. But you still have to do the work, just differently.

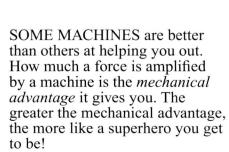

SOME MACHINES are better than others at helping you out. How much a force is amplified by a machine is the *mechanical advantage* it gives you. The greater the mechanical advantage, the more like a superhero you get to be!

It's Simple!

You might usually think of a machine as a complicated metal thing with lots of moving parts, like a car or a washing machine. But to physicists it can be something much simpler than that.

It doesn't need to be complicated, or metal, and it doesn't even need to have any parts that move on their own.

There are five types of simple machine, meaning basic mechanical devices that help to apply a force. We use them every day in lots of different ways. They are: lever, pulley, screw, wheel and axle, and wedge and inclined plane.

EVEN A THUMBTACK is a simple machine!

Top Tip

Keep your bicycle, scooter, skateboard, or roller skates well-oiled so the parts move smoothly with little friction.

LOTS OF simple machines don't look like "machines" at all. A spade is a machine; so is the screw lid of a jar, a nail, a hammer, and even a plank balanced on a log.

FRICTION IS a force that operates between moving surfaces. Rougher surfaces produce more friction. Friction produces heat—that's why rubbing your hands together warms them up, and why working machines get hot.

SIMPLE machines can be combined to make a compound machine. These can be very complicated, like an oil rig or a racing car.

SOME MACHINES work more effectively than our bodies, wasting less energy as heat. A bicycle uses the work of your muscles more efficiently than running.

Putting Machines to Work

Our earliest ancestors must have discovered some simple machines while still living in caves. Other simple machines, such as wheels and pulleys, need to be made deliberately and would have come later. Simple machines made human civilization possible. They enabled people to make buildings, dig the soil, water crops, move around, make fabrics and tools, and even fight each other.

USING A STRONG stick as a lever makes it very easy to move a really heavy stone. Look out below!

SOME simple machines are so obvious, even animals use them. Some birds use sticks as levers. The nuthatch uses one to lift tree bark to uncover insects hidden beneath.

Something's not right . . .

A SHADOOF consists of a bucket attached to a stick that pivots so that the water can be scooped up. Without watering crops with tools like this, human civilization would never have taken off!

It's easier to move something up a slope than to lift it straight up, and it's safer to move something down a slope than to drop it off an edge.

WHEELS were invented in several places around the same time, about 5,500 years ago. They made it much easier to move things and people.

WEDGES, ramps, levers, and pulleys helped people to build huge structures such as Stonehenge in England and the pyramids in Egypt.

ARCHIMEDES' screw has been used for at least 2,700 years for raising water. Turning the screw scoops up water and brings it up along the shaft.

A PLOWHSHARE is a wedge that cuts through the soil, making a furrow (dip) in which seed can be sown in a nice neat row. Plows have been used for 5,500 years.

So much faster than a bucket!

11

It's Not All Fun and Games

A lever is essentially some type of stick used in a useful way. It uses your effort to move a load, but translates a large movement into a small one. This means that you can move a lighter thing over a large distance, and the lever converts that into moving a heavier thing a short distance. Without simple machines like levers, we'd never be able to move anything heavier than we can lift or push. Imagine all the things we couldn't do!

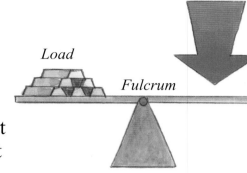

Effort

Load

Fulcrum

LEVERS USE effort exerted at one point to move a load at another point. The point around which the lever moves is called the fulcrum.

We'll have to go back!

Make a model seesaw and experiment with varying the positions and size of the load and effort. What happens if you move the fulcrum toward one end?

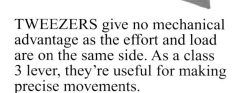

A SEESAW is a class 1 lever. Each person on a seesaw provides both load and effort. More effort on one side can raise the load too much!

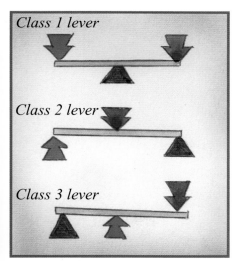

Class 1 lever

Class 2 lever

Class 3 lever

THERE ARE three types of lever. They vary according to where the fulcrum is in relation to the lever. You can find out more about them on pages 33 and 35.

TWEEZERS give no mechanical advantage as the effort and load are on the same side. As a class 3 lever, they're useful for making precise movements.

JAWS are a pair of levers that work together, like super-snappy scissors. The two jaws exert force in opposite directions.

A WHEELBARROW is a class 2 lever. The effort and load both move in the same direction—up.

13

The Wheels on the Bus

Wheels are easier to recognize as simple machines than some other simple machines. One or more wheels are attached at the center to a rod (called the axle), so that both the wheel and the axle turn together. Wheels and axles can work in either of two ways. We can apply a force to the rim of the wheel to turn the axle, or we can apply a force to the axle to turn the wheel. Wheels often come in pairs, one at each end of an axle.

IT'S EASIER to move a box on a cart than to drag it over the ground. Wheels reduce the area in contact with the ground, so there is less friction.

THE OUTSIDE of a wheel moves much farther than the center. The bigger the wheel, the farther the vehicle moves with each turn.

I'm winning!

Use a construction toy to make a vehicle with wheels and axles. If you have a variety of wheels, experiment with different sizes.

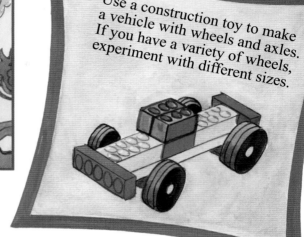

A MERRY-GO-ROUND is a giant wheel-and-axle system. The middle turns more slowly than the outside, so don't choose a ride near the edge unless you like to go fast!

COGS OR GEARS are wheels with teeth that lock into the teeth of another wheel. When one turns, it turns another. With these, the turning rim of one wheel turns the rim of another.

THE INVENTION of the wheel made people more productive. A horse-drawn wagon can move 10 times as much as a person carrying a load, over the same distance in the same amount of time.

THE PEOPLE of the early civilizations in South America lived without wheels. Perhaps they didn't invent wheels because they had no large, strong animals to pull carts!

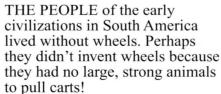

15

Ups and Downs

A pulley is a combination of a rope and a grooved wheel, used for moving things up and down. A load is attached to the rope, which runs over the wheel. Pulling on the end of the rope lifts the weight.

A pulley is a special way of using a wheel and axle. As the wheel turns on its axle, its movement is transferred to the rope that runs over the rim of the wheel. A pulley changes the direction of a force. It's usually easier to pull downward than to lift a load upward.

BUILDING SITES are a good place to spot pulleys in action. They're used to lift heavy materials up to where construction workers need them.

How It Works

Older elevators work using a pulley. A counterweight balances the weight of the elevator and as one goes up, the other goes down.

A SIMPLE pulley doesn't reduce the effort needed to move a load, but it makes a task feel easier.

SAILORS move heavy sails using a block and tackle system—two or more linked pulleys with a rope running through both. Without pulleys, sailing ships could only go as far as people could row.

PULLEYS ARE used to haul water from a well. It's easier to pull a rope over a pulley than just to pull it over a beam or branch, because there's less friction. And it's a lot easier than climbing down to the water every time.

A Slippery Slope

A wedge is a shaped block that's forced between two objects to separate them. The first wedges were used thousands of years ago. Wedges can have a single slanting face or two slanting faces (a double wedge). Force applied to the fat end of the wedge is translated into force at right angles to the sloped surface of the wedge. A ramp or inclined plane is one face of a wedge. It's often used to make it easier to move something up or down. If you whiz down a slide, you're having fun with an inclined plane!

A NARROW wedge is easier to drive into a small gap—but it has to move farther to have the same effect as a wider wedge.

WEDGES HAVE been used for thousands of years for breaking apart tough materials. The Egyptian pyramids couldn't have been built without them!

The wheels of a wheelchair or baby stroller push (exert a force) downward and forward. This won't take the vehicle up a step, but easily moves it along the sloping surface of a ramp.

MOST CUTTING tools are wedges. They slide between particles of material where a blunt edge would just crush the matter beneath it.

WOODEN wedges driven into rock and soaked with water were once used to split rock. The wedge swells, forcing the rock apart. If the water freezes, it works even better—ice takes up more space than the same weight of water, so the wedge grows larger.

WEDGES can also be used to keep things in place. A doorstop is a wedge that sits between the floor and the bottom of the door. A nail is a wedge that pushes apart the surface of a wall or piece of wood.

YOUR MOUTH is full of wedges—look at the shape of your front teeth! Jaw muscles force your wedge-teeth into food, breaking it apart.

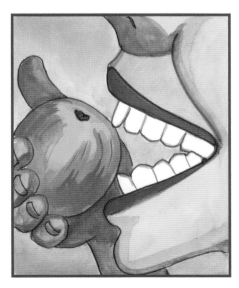

All Screwed Up

A screw is a tiny inclined plane wound around a shaft. It changes rotational (round and round) movement to linear (straight line) movement. Turning a screw moves its shaft in a straight line. You can see how this works every time you use a screwdriver: You turn the screwdriver, which turns the screw, which moves forward (into) or backward (out of) whatever you are screwing into. A screw doesn't need to look like a screw. The thread can be on the outside (as it is on a screw) or it can be on the inside (as it is on the lid of a jar).

THE THREAD of a wood screw is sharp at its edge. This acts like a blade or wedge, pushing its way into the wood. The rest of the curly wedge helps to push it forward. If it meets something too hard, the screw locks—it doesn't go backward.

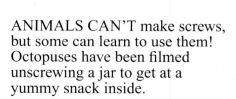

ANIMALS CAN'T make screws, but some can learn to use them! Octopuses have been filmed unscrewing a jar to get at a yummy snack inside.

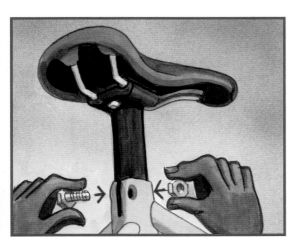

SCREWS WORK alone, but bolts always work in a pair with nuts. You need to put a bolt into a hole and then screw a nut with a matching thread onto the end.

Top Tip

Screws work two ways. You can take them out after you've put them in. That means you can take things apart again. It's much harder to take apart something put together with nails.

A CAR JACK uses a screw to separate things—the car from the road surface. How would you change a tire if you couldn't lift the car? The jack makes it simple. Your muscle power is enough to turn a screw that separates the arms of the jack, and the car on top is pushed upward. Easy!

IF ALL SCREWS suddenly vanished, lots of things would just fall apart: furniture, buildings, vehicles. Screws might normally be hidden, but they serve a really useful purpose.

Oh no!

SCREWS CAN BE used to pull two surfaces together and crush or press whatever is between them. In a press used to make olive oil or wine, a huge screw is used to lower a wide, flat plate into a barrel of olives or grapes, squashing them until the juice leaks out.

21

Putting It Together

Simple machines aren't just used on their own. A complex—or compound—machine is made from simple machines working together. It can use just a few simple machines, or hundreds, as components.

Compound machines can amplify a force, change the direction of a force, change the type of energy, and change the type of motion. They can change one kind of motion into another, sometimes going through several other kinds of motion on the way. There are four types of motion: linear, rotary, reciprocating, and oscillating.

LINEAR MOTION is movement in a straight line, like a toy car moving forward.

A BICYCLE is a compound machine. The gears transfer motion to the wheels. They go around (rotary motion) and the bicycle goes forward (linear motion).

THE BRAKES are levers. They move the brake blocks against the wheel (a linear movement) to stop the rotary motion of the wheel.

ROTARY (round and round) motion goes in circles, like the wheel of a unicycle. The cyclist presses down on the pedals to turn the wheel.

Every compound machine has a source of energy, and mechanisms to produce and change forces and motions. Most machines also have some kind of user interface.

RECIPROCATING motion goes backward and forward, like a saw cutting through wood. The teeth of the saw are tiny wedges that force their way into the wood.

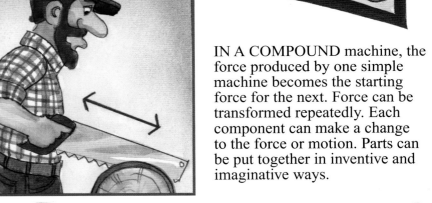

IN A COMPOUND machine, the force produced by one simple machine becomes the starting force for the next. Force can be transformed repeatedly. Each component can make a change to the force or motion. Parts can be put together in inventive and imaginative ways.

OSCILLATING motion is swinging from side to side, like a pendulum in a clock. Oscillating motion can be fun!

23

World-Changing Machines

Simple machines helped people to farm, build, and make societies. They got us started! No one needed to understand how levers, wheels, and wedges worked in order to use them. But then scientists and engineers began to explore and investigate machines. And soon, understanding how machines worked and putting them together into compound machines revolutionized societies. Without machines, we would have none of the benefits of farming and industrialization. Life would be very different.

Just taking the next batch to market!

PRINTING PRESS INVENTED!

THE INVENTION of the printing press around 1440 made books easily available, and knowledge soon spread rapidly. Without levers and screws, all books would still be handwritten.

CLOCKWORK is used for clocks and mechanisms, including automata and toys. Without wheels for clockwork, our ancestors would not have been able to measure time accurately.

INVENTED in India 1,000 years ago, a spinning wheel pulls yarn from a bundle of wool. The Spinning Jenny (1764) could make many threads at once, which revolutionized fabric making.

WINDMILL

Wind

Rotation

Grain fed in

Floating stone

Rotary stone

Drive shaft

THE WIND turns a windmill's sails, attached to a shaft, which turns a gear, which turns a spindle at right angles to it. That turns another shaft, which turns a stone. Windmills ground corn and wheat, so people could make bread.

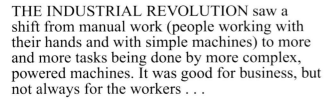

THE INDUSTRIAL REVOLUTION saw a shift from manual work (people working with their hands and with simple machines) to more and more tasks being done by more complex, powered machines. It was good for business, but not always for the workers . . .

. . . MANY PEOPLE rebelled against machines taking their jobs and making their skills less valuable. Some workers even attacked and broke up compound machines, but they needed to use simple machines to do so!

25

Power to the People

The first machines were powered by human or animal muscle power, or by the energy of wind or moving water. During the Industrial Revolution, extra power sources became available. Earlier machines were replaced by engines driven by steam, fuel, and electricity. People (and animals) had to do a lot less physical work, and the new machines were faster and more efficient. They didn't get tired, need to sleep, get sick, or go on vacation. Industry became much more productive, and societies flourished.

A WAGON and a train both use wheels, but a train can do much more work because it has more energy available to it.

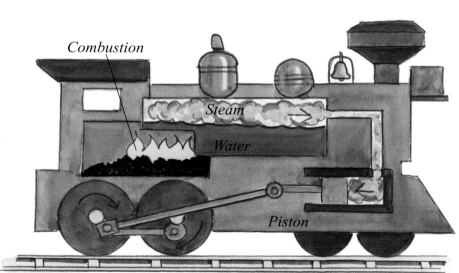

Combustion

Steam

Water

Piston

THE INDUSTRIAL REVOLUTION was largely powered by steam. The energy for a steam train comes from the pressure of boiling water in a closed space so that it pushes a piston. A steam train burned coal to heat water and provide steam pressure. This then drove pistons attached to cranks and transferred movement to the wheels, moving the train along.

THE INTERNAL combustion engine (used in motor vehicles) takes energy from burning liquid fuel in a small space, using the pressure to drive a piston and so eventually turn the wheels.

How It Works

We make electricity by turning a dense metal coil inside a magnetic field. When you use a windup flashlight, you're doing that directly. The electricity you make is stored in a battery.

ALESSANDRO Volta developed the first battery to produce electricity in 1799. Now lots of machines are powered by batteries. Imagine how different life would be without electricity!

POWER makes compound machines much more useful—but without simple machines, there wouldn't be any powered machines. We wouldn't be left with many transportation options.

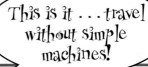

This is it . . . travel without simple machines!

Would You Want to Live Without Simple Machines?

If all the simple machines vanished overnight, there wouldn't be much technology left. Even things that aren't simple machines themselves are made using simple machines. We would have to find new—or old—ways of doing things that we currently take for granted. Life wouldn't be impossible, but it would be very different.

Luckily, simple machines aren't about to disappear. Instead, we will continue to find more and more ingenious and exciting uses for them.

WE DON'T notice some of the simple machines around us. The pointy nose of a fast train is a wedge, allowing it to move through the air much faster.

SIMPLE machines are all around us every day. Imagine how different life would be if we had to give them up.

Try to keep track of all the machines and simple machines you use in the course of a day. It will be a long list! Start with your toothbrush. . . .

MOST OF our vehicles use wheels and axles, and even those that don't run on wheels use levers and pulleys for steering. What would you think about riding a donkey to school? What would the donkey do all day?

SIMPLE machines are being put to more and more complex uses. Without them, we wouldn't be making any technological progress. Who knows what they will be used for next?

MACHINES ARE taking over many difficult tasks. A bridge that began construction in Amsterdam, Holland, in 2016, was put together entirely by robots from parts produced in metal using a 3-D printer.

LOTS OF TOYS and activities depend on simple machines: merry-go-rounds, Ferris wheels, seesaws, swings, slides, roller blades, skateboards, and more.

SOME MACHINES seem to have hardly any mechanical parts. But simple machines are still needed to make them. There's no getting away from simple machines in the end!

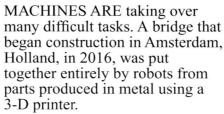

29

Glossary

Amplify To make larger.

Automata (singular: automaton) Mechanical moving figures.

Axle The rod that runs through the middle of one or more wheels, providing the movement that turns the wheels.

Car jack A tool for lifting part of a car off the ground.

Civilization The most advanced form of organized society, characterized by people building cities, developing communal projects, and achieving advanced progress in science, technology, and arts.

Compound machine A machine that has two or more simple machines among its components. An automobile is a good example.

Counterweight A heavy object that balances the weight of another part of a system.

Effort A force exerted by a machine or a person using a machine.

Force A push or a pull on an object, coming from its interaction with another object (or person).

Friction The force operating between two objects trying to move against each other. Friction resists movement and causes some of the energy in the system to be wasted as heat.

Fulcrum The pivoting or balancing point in a lever.

Inclined Slanted or tilted.

Industrial Revolution A period from around 1760 to 1830 which saw a very rapid increase in mechanization and factory-building. People moved from manual work in small-scale industries to operating machines in large-scale industries, often leaving the countryside to live in cities.

Ingenious Clever and original.

Internal combustion engine An engine that burns fuel inside a sealed compartment, using the resulting pressure to move a piston.

Linear motion A movement in a straight line.

Load The weight that a machine is trying to move.

Mechanical Operated by some kind of machine.

Mechanical advantage The benefit gained by using a machine to do a task, measured as the force produced by a machine relative to the force applied to it.

Piston A plunger that fits closely inside a sealed compartment, moved by the pressure of compressed liquid or gas.

Printing press A machine that prints documents by pressing inked metal letters against a piece of paper.

Reciprocating motion A movement backward and forward.

Rotary motion A movement in circles, such as a wheel going around.

Shaft A long rod or pole to which something is fastened, or which forms the central part of a structure.

Stonehenge A circular structure made of huge chunks of shaped stone, some upright and some lying across the top of the uprights. It is near Salisbury in England, and was started around 5,100 years ago.

3-D printer A printer that makes a three-dimensional object, usually from plastic or metal.

Translate Convert into a different form or direction.

Work The process of transferring energy from one form or place to another.

Index

Amazing Simple Machines

Simple machines are so versatile that tools that look very similar can have very different uses. Think of a pair of scissors, a pair of pliers, and a pair of tweezers: The basic design is similar, but we put them to completely different uses!

A pair of scissors is not one simple machine, but two different simple machines combined—a compound machine. Each blade is a wedge, but it's also working as a lever. The fulcrum is the point where the blades join. When you bring the handles of the scissors together, the force pushes the blades together to make the cut.

A pair of pliers has blunt ends instead of blades. Pliers have longer arms for the handle and shorter arms for the wedges. You make a large movement with your hand, which puts a lot of force into a small movement, enabling a strong grip.

Tweezers have the fulcrum at one end instead of the middle. They are useful when you don't need to use of lot of force, but want to make a precise movement. Because of the location of the fulcrum, the tweezers don't amplify the force you apply.

Five Top Uses for Simple Machines

Opening and closing things. You use a simple machine whenever you use a screw-top lid, on drink bottles, toothpaste tubes, shampoo bottles, and a hundred other things.

Levering things. Whenever you use a screwdriver or coin to open the battery compartment of a toy, you're using a lever.

Moving! We use wheels and axles all the time, from bicycles to buses and trains to carts. On a car or a bus, the wheels aren't just on the outside: The steering wheel is another wheel, and the cogs and gears inside the engine are wheels, too.

Cutting things. Almost everything you cut, you cut with a wedge: the knife you use for your food, the scissors you use for paper and fabric, and even the teeth in your mouth. Wedges push through tough or flexible stuff by forcing a way between the fibers or particles.

Holding things together. If you tack a picture to a wall, the tack is a wedge; if you nail something together, the nail is a wedge; if you screw something together, the screw is—obviously—a screw!